YOUR GOD PATH

Practical Ways to Live the Best
Moments in Your Life

————— ◆ —————

THOMAS S. ROBINSON

Your God Path
Practical Ways to Live the Best Moments in Your Life

iUniverse books may be ordered through booksellers or by contacting:

iUniverse
1663 Liberty Drive
Bloomington, IN 47403
www.iuniverse.com
1-800-Authors (1-800-288-4677)

The Holy Bible, Modern English Version. © 2014 by Military Bible Association. Published and distributed by Charisma House.

New Century Version® ©2005 Thomas Nelson Inc. publishers
New American Standard Bible c. 1995 The Lockman Foundation
English Standard Version. ESV® Text Edition: 2016. Copyright © 2001 by Crossway Bibles, a publishing ministry of Good News Publishers.

New Revised Standard Version

ISBN: 978-1-5320-8342-6 (sc)
ISBN: 978-1-5320-8343-3 (e)

Library of Congress Control Number: 2019914360

Print information available on the last page.

iUniverse rev. date: 10/03/2019

CONTENTS

To several people who encouraged me to follow my dream to write this book.

First to my wife, Jane, who has believed in me and trusted in me since we were fifteen-year-old high school kids.

Then to my friend, Bonnie Hapstack, for showing me that God is always doing something, even when I am not seeing it myself.

And last, but not least, my mother and father, the late Dolores and Thomas Robinson Jr., who raised me with a tremendous amount of courage to try new things.

In this book I have made use of several versions of biblical texts when using direct quotations. I invite you to compare these versions with others you may have. I predominantly use the New Revised Standard Version for my own reading, but supplement that with other versions in this book. These include the Modern English Version (MEV), the New American Standard Bible (NASB), the English Standard Version (ESV), and the New Century Version (NCV).

INTRODUCTION

My brother, Greg, and his wife, Kerri, recently took some vacation time in the Hawaiian islands, specifically, on Maui. On one particular day, he was texting me some pictures and describing a day trip that he and his wife were on at that moment. Modern technology! They were taking the road to Hana, and he explained that the journey was not about getting to Hana, but about the *road* they were taking to get there. It wasn't about arriving, but about experiencing the journey they traveled. Curious, I looked it up online and read about some of the experiences they were having: Twin Falls, the Garden of Eden Arboretum, Wailua Valley, Lava Tube Beaches, Kahanu Garden, and several other sights to stop and experience as they followed this road.

Then it hit me: this is life! We may all have a destination, but the journey there is just as important as is this destination! If my brother and his wife focused on just reaching Hana, not only would they have missed a great many beautiful and wondrous experiences along the way, but also they may have found that Hana was not the best part of the journey. Our life is not about where we end up as much as it is about what we experience while we live it. Before Jesus died on the cross, he lived! He walked and ate and laughed and wept. He lived each day and experienced joys and sorrows, aggravation and jubilation. He did not rush headlong to the cross but lived each day with fullness. He lived every day of the roughly twelve thousand days of his thirty-three years on this earth.

What I want to lay out for you are some practical concepts about living each day of your life. I'll share some of real experiences we all face in life and how these experiences are powerful tools for our living our very best moments in those times. It's my belief that when you live each day in the moment, you're learning to walk with God, and so I call this our God Path.

The concluding words of David's sixteenth song proclaim:

> You will make known to me the path of life; in Your presence is fullness of joy; at Your right hand there are pleasures for evermore.

—Psalm 16:11[1]

Let's discover this "path of life" that brings us into the presence of God while it opens each day to a grand adventure.

---

[1] MEV

CHAPTER 1

THE QUESTION IS THE ANSWER

Pablo Picasso once remarked, "Computers are useless. They can only give you answers." As a creative person, Picasso was fascinated with the great questions. The questions were important to people like him because the questions empowered them to seek after answers which led to greater truth. For Picasso and others like him, it wasn't about instant gratification and quick answers to relatively unimportant questions. It was about the journey itself as one sought to go deeper into even larger questions of life.

Jesus the Nazarene loved the journey. His answers to the questions people asked of him were usually delivered in a parable or some other puzzle that invited the person to join in the journey. He understood the best answer is not the one given but the one *discovered* by the person seeking the answer.

An example of this occurs one day when a scribe asks Jesus, "Who is my neighbor?"[2] Rather than giving a direct answer, Jesus tells the story of a man beaten and left for dead and the reactions of three different people to the man. He then asks at the end of the parable, "Now which of these three do you think was a neighbor to him who fell among the thieves?" He allows the scribe to draw his own conclusion.

Another good example of this in found among his own disciples. The disciples are arguing about who is the greatest disciple of Jesus. He directs their attention to a little child and makes them ponder the meaning of true greatness.[3]

---

[2] See Luke 10:29
[3] See Luke 9:46–48

Some try to trap him and ruin his reputation, asking about paying taxes. Jesus responds with a question asking whose image is on the coin.[4] It's their answer to Jesus's question that provides him with the response that challenges their perspective!

I first experienced the power and wisdom in this when I was about seventeen years old. A woman in my church was leading a few of us in a Bible study about Jesus's resurrected appearance to Mary Magdalene in the garden. We were asked why Jesus wouldn't allow Mary to touch him. It was a question of "why"—why did one person act in a way that seemed so different than most people would have acted? It immediately changed the focus of the passage for me as I was confronted with looking at an event from a different perspective. I was forced into the person's mind, into his life and his world. My perspective broadened, and I found myself discovering a world outside my own. It all started with a simple yet potent question.

Think back on some of the teachers you admire and from whom you learned the most. Chances are good that they were gifted in helping you discover the answers for yourself rather than just giving them directly to you.

Perhaps this is why the Bible, rather than uniting Christians, so often divides us. Our attempts to use it as a simple "answer book" to our questions only serves to place us into separate camps of interpretation. We find ourselves confused, choosing sides and becoming critical of those who don't see it our way. The quest for answers leads us into various heated debates on what is the truth. One's perception makes a world of difference.

Picture a soda can suspended a few feet away from a corner in your home. If you were to only view that can from the side, you would claim the shape of the can is a rectangle. You would offer proof by shining a light at the can from your position which would cast a rectangular shadow on the wall behind it. Now say I am looking at the can from the top side of the can. All I can see is a circle. I argue that the can is a circle, and prove it by shining a light from my position, which casts a circular shadow on the wall from my position. We are both expressing a truth about the can, but our truths are only partial truths. We are limiting ourselves from the full truth by not looking at the can from different positions.

I believe there are two divine purposes for the Bible's ambiguity. The first divine purpose is God's desire to be in relationship with us. When we are confronted by scriptural texts that seem contradictory, we need to then go to the source for help. We need to consult the source of those texts. While God did not actually handwrite the Bible, but did inspire many authors to write from

---

[4] See Mark 12:16

their perspectives with the guidance of the Holy Spirit (again, this is one belief and so it is taken on faith), we cannot actually interview the human authors on what they wrote. However, we can seek wisdom from a more spiritual source of truth. Moreover, we have the help of many biblical scholars who can add to our understanding of the context in which the words of Scripture were written. Reading the biblical story of the fall of Sodom in Genesis, for example, can be seen from its surface as God's judgment on a city of people who committed a sexually perverse act. We can take away an assumption that God punished the people of Sodom for that act, as many have done. However, the Lord proclaims through the prophet Ezekiel the sin of Sodom is something much different:

> This was the sin of your sister Sodom: She and her daughters were proud and had plenty of food and lived in great comfort, but she did not help the poor and needy. -Ezekiel 16:49[5]

Moreover, through scholarly research, we learn there was a law of hospitality to be observed by people in that time. While we think of hospitality as providing food, comfort, and perhaps entertainment for guests, the ancient world was harsh and deadly. The traveler who moved about because of business had to traverse desert places where water and food were vital for survival. Cities and villages were often built around the sparse watering holes and wells found in these desert places. Therefore, the traveler was dependent on the welcome and hospitality of these places for his very life. The cities and villages were expected to be kind and generous to the traveler and, in return, expected to be honored for their hospitality from harm or theft. These customs were not informal, but had become a formal and sacred code of conduct. They were considered the very will of God written into the laws. Abraham's welcome of the three strangers is an example of the proper way to welcome and treat a traveler.

The sexual act the inhabitants of Sodom desired to inflict on the two strangers in Lot's home was not an act of homosexuality. It is an act of violence and a contempt for the Law. The act was a rape meant to humiliate and degrade these men, much the way men in prison may rape and humiliate a new prisoner to establish dominance and contempt. Lot's offering of his daughters in place of the two men under his roof and protection reveals how deeply he holds to the Law and the sacrifice he is willing to make to uphold it.

---

[5] NCV

This is why we need more than the Bible to know God. The Bible is a collection of several dozen books written by many different authors, many unknown, and covering a time frame of several thousand years. One author writes to sacrifice animals to please the Lord,[6] and another writes that God is not pleased with burnt offerings at all.[7] The earliest gospel, Mark, says that three women went to the tomb of Jesus. Mark names them as Mary Magdalene; Mary, the mother of James; and Salome.[8] Matthew's gospel says there were two women: Mary Magdalene and the other Mary.[9] Luke's gospel is unclear on the number of women. He eventually names Mary Magdalene, Joanna, Mary (the mother of James), "and the other women."[10] John's gospel, the last of the four gospels written, has only one woman who ventured there: Mary Magdalene.[11] These variations are why we need to have a relationship with God himself. We are not to worship the Bible, but the God who is the one constant person throughout the biblical books.

The second reason, I believe, that the Bible is not as perfectly clear as many people would like it to be is this: God wants us to be on the journey—seeking God and the answers out in life!

I've often shared that, for me, the Bible is like a map. In times long before computers and global positioning systems (GPS) that use satellites and technology, explorers would take journeys and create maps for others to follow to know the land and the sea, to know what the journey would hold. Maps would contain information of where dangers were likely to be found, where safe passage would be located, and help those who followed to make their way. The Bible is our spiritual map created by those who have explored the spiritual life for themselves. It holds the stories of their pitfalls and lessons learned in their walks with God on the path of life. It has been preserved for us to study and learn. And then we must get up and take our own journey with God. We cannot truly know God from the book alone. We'll not truly know ourselves from merely reading the "map" and staying safely tucked away in our church pews.

Want to love your enemies as Jesus commanded? The answer isn't found in a book but instead, is discovered in talking to them, listening to their stories, relating to them.

---

[6] See Leviticus 3
[7] See Hosea 6:6
[8] See Mark 16:1.
[9] See Matthew 28:1.
[10] See Luke 24:10.
[11] See John 20:1.

Want to be a "neighbor" to people in need? It won't happen by hiding in your home and reading about it in the Bible. You need to step out into the community and meet them, show an interest in them, and learn their struggles.

Jesus leads by example. He gets out there and meets people and hears their stories and shares himself with them.

As we continue this journey, consider this story about where we may fail when we seek God and God's truth:

> A neighbor found Jack on his hands and knees.
> He asked, "What are you searching for, Jack?"
> "My key."
> Both men got on their knees to search.
> After a while the neighbor asked, "Where did you lose it?"
> "At home."
> "Good Lord! Then why are you searching here?"
> "Because it's brighter here."

Now Consider This

What is that one important question you have that's continued to irritate you? Is it because you are afraid that you already know the answer? Is it a battle between your mind and your heart? Is it a war between what you think the Bible says and what you think God would say to you today?

CHAPTER 2

LOVE LETS GO

While listening to a Christian radio station one morning on my drive to the office, I heard one of the on-air personalities share his thoughts on how Jesus let people walk away from him. He remarked, "If I were Jesus, I would have used my powers to make people stay and listen to me. But Jesus didn't. He let people who wanted to walk away from him just walk away!"

That's a powerful word for us. We all have people in our lives whom we bend over backward, trying to keep them around. For some reason, we'll let certain people walk all over us because we fear losing them. Maybe we need to take a little time in prayer and meditation and ask ourselves why.

Jesus's reason for letting people walk away was that he respected our free will so much he would not infringe upon it. He valued this gift of freedom that God had bestowed upon us that he would not use his power to interfere with this gift.

One day, a rich young man came running up to Jesus and knelt before him, asking how he might earn eternal life: "Good teacher, what must I do to inherit eternal life?"[12] Notice this man's belief system as revealed by his words *do* and *inherit"* He asks what he must *do*, not what he must *believe* or *who* he must know.

We're a society that has leaned heavily on the philosophy that one must *earn* what one receives. It's based solidly on the concept of being deserving by one's actions. Yet in the society in which Jesus lived, people were accustomed to receiving things by virtue of the station in life into which they had been born and who that status afforded them the benefit of knowing.

---

[12] See Mark 10:17–22

Rich people, like this young man, had inherited their wealth by virtue of the family into which they were born. Deuteronomic law states that the firstborn son receives a double portion of the inheritance.[13] Thus, if there are two brothers, the elder received about 66 percent, and the younger received the remaining percentage. Three brothers would be divided up as 50%, 25% and 25%. The reasoning behind the elder's larger inheritance was based on the extra responsibilities he would now take on as the eldest. He would be expected to take over the family business his father had been running. In the book of Numbers, chapter 27, there's a prescribed ranking of how any property was to be distributed through the family. So since the law of inheritance was pretty well spelled out, what is this rich young man really thinking when he asks about inheriting eternal life?

The laws were clear for real property here in this life, but what's the secret, the procedure, the ranking system, for someone to inherit eternal life?

Jesus responds directly to the man's philosophy of this concept of "earning" eternal life, telling the man that he already knows the commandments, specifically naming the six that focus on our relationships with others: murder, adultery, stealing, bearing false witness, fraud, and honoring our parents.[14]

Jesus points to the commandments, in what may well be a sarcastic tone of voice, as the path to "earn" the inheritance. It's as if Jesus says, "Well, if you want to 'earn' an eternal life, then follow all the commandments."

But the young man wasn't satisfied, believing he has somehow accomplished this great feat, and realizes in his heart that it doesn't seem to be good enough. Jesus then "looking at him, loved him." I believe Jesus loves him because he recognizes how truly young and naïve this man is. He sees how hard this man is trying to get his life right with God in a sincere way. So Jesus then tells him the only thing in the young man's way is his wealth. And the young man walks away—and Jesus lets him go. He could have chased after him, explained the concept of grace, or told the boy he was kidding. But Jesus let him walk away.

Jesus's heart ached for that young man. As he watched the young fellow walk away, Jesus was questioned by his disciples. They were apparently dumbfounded that the rich young man is unable to earn his way into eternal life. From the traditions and teachings of their faith, this man represented the best of God's children. His faithfulness and dedication to fulfilling God's

---

[13] See Deuteronomy 21:17
[14] See Mark 10:19

commandments surely had resulted in his wealth as a blessing from God. If he couldn't earn eternal life, who in this world could? Jesus sought to enlighten them, pointing out that this may be impossible on our own, but nothing is impossible with God's help.[15]

So Jesus, loving this young man, let him walk away. He didn't chase after him. He didn't plead with him to reconsider. He loved the man, dished out the truth to him, and let him walk away. Jesus gave the young man over to his Father and returned to the path he was walking. He had a lot of work to do. As the educator Melvin Chapman once said, "You can't please everybody if you are going to make a difference in this world."[16]

You have a mission. You have a path God is calling you to walk. It's a lot of work for you. And you have to be as respectful to those who disagree with you, as Jesus was, and let them walk away if they so choose. Sometimes, that's a heartbreaking thing to do.

NOW CONSIDER THIS

Is there someone you've been expending far too much energy and time on? Maybe God is saying to you, "Let them walk away now. I'll take over from here."

---

[15] See Mark 10:27

[16] https://www.bannerview.com/blog/jhelvin/BOSVIEW/Where-Does-the-Time-Go/

CHAPTER 3

STAY FOCUSED ON YOUR GOAL

Obstacles are a given on the God Path. Many people view obstacles as dead ends. They're the places many people give up on their dreams and goals. They turn back toward their comfort zones. Then they spend the rest of their lives sitting around telling others how they met too much resistance to their dreams and settled for something less than they wanted out of life.

The next time you're faced with a seemingly insurmountable task, consider the hurdles Erik Weihenmayer has overcome. Erik has worked as a middle school teacher, run marathons, and performed acrobatic skydiving stunts. He's also a scuba diver, downhill skier, and long-distance bicyclist. Those are impressive accomplishments for any forty-seven-year old. However, Erik has been blind since age thirteen when a degenerative eye disease destroyed his retinas.

Being blind has not prevented him from embracing all life has to offer. He hit a personal high goal at age thirty-two in 2001 by becoming the first blind climber to reach the top of Mount Everest. This is the tallest challenge in the world for *any* mountaineer. Erik's belief is that "a spark of greatness exists in all people, but only by touching that spark to adversity's flame does it blaze into the force that fuels our lives and the world."[17]

Jesus revealed that this was true for him as well. The greatness that was within him needed to be prepared for a brighter blaze to challenge and change the world. So, immediately following his baptism by John, the Spirit compelled him into the worlderness for a time of testing through adverstity.

---

[17] Erik's quote is found on his website www.touchthetop.com.

The temptation Jesus faced in the wilderness included attacks on his hunger, going for the quick fix Band-Aid approach, exhibits of power, feeding his ego, and taking the well-traveled path of ease.

Matthew and Luke chose to add this event in Jesus's life to their gospels for an important reason. On the surface, it may be that they wanted to show us the strength of Jesus's character to be the Messiah. I also believe that they wanted to help their readers recognize that the God Path is not an open and clear road for anyone, not even for the Messiah. Obstacles are not a punishment or a deterent for the traveler, but are a means of building the traveler's spirit and bringing greater truth into the traveler's heart and soul.

As Jesus comes to the end of his time in the wilderness, the tempter speaks to him. The tempter knows what Jesus feels because the tempter is in our own minds. While Matthew and Luke may designate the tempter as the Devil, you and I know there's no need for an outside influence to utter these temptations. We all know how well our own fears and doubts can creep in and take over our thoughts. At the very foundation of each of the first two temptations Jesus endures is the obstacle of doubt and trust. The tempter starts each remark with "if you are God's Son."[18] This is a direct shot at Jesus's identity. "Am I who I believe I am? Am I truly God's beloved, or am I delusional, a madman?" Self-doubt is a powerful obstacle to reaching one's goals. If Jesus begins to question his relationship with God, if he begins to lose faith in himself and God, he will lose conviction for his journey. The gospels show us that Jesus not only holds onto his identity and his faith in God, but also strengthens it by resisting the temptation to prove his identity and faith.

When a CNN interviewer asked Erik Weihenmayer what he did to keep his faith in himself and accomplish his goal of climbing Mount Everest, he replied, "I just kept telling myself: 'Be focused. Be full of energy. Keep relaxed. Don't let all those distractions—the fear and the doubts—creep into your brain, because that's what ruins you up there.'" He then pointed to his *head*.

On Erik's website (*touchthetop.com*) he shares his latest adventure: solo kayaking the Grand Canyon.

---

[18] See Matthew 4:3, 6

From September 7–28, 2014, I tackled another historic challenge: solo kayaking the Grand Canyon 277 miles, from Lee's Ferry to Pearce Ferry. Joining me was blind Navy veteran and accomplished kayaker Lonnie Bedwell. Together, we made a powerful and authentic statement about living a *No Barriers Life* and the belief that this was possible for each of us. Sponsoring the expedition was Nature Valley, reinforcing its own campaign theme: "Feel Nature's Energy." The expedition was hosted by *No Barriers USA*, a nonprofit organization that empowers people with the message, "What's within you is stronger than what's in your way.

Erik doesn't accomplish goals by being faster or busier than other people. He accomplishes them by being more focused and more determined. You and I can learn a lot from him.

NOW CONSIDER THIS

What's the goal on your God Path? Are you ready to give it 100 percent of your attention and go toward it?

CHAPTER 4

A "Mad Lib" Influence

I recently received a surprise card in the mail from my cousin, Linda, whom I haven't seen in a very, very long time. Linda and I were the closest of all my cousins (and I had twenty-four cousins on my dad's side and one on my mom's). She and I had similar senses of humor, and enjoyed many of the same activities. The card was an Easter card, and she wrote that I was an important part of her life and thanked me.

At first, I thought it odd since I've hardly been in communication with her since we were young kids. We reconnected a little on Facebook, but our communication is generally a once-a-year Christmas card. However, as I thought about it, I realized that she had truly had a huge impact on my life. She was the one who turned me on to the *Mad Libs* books as a kid. Because of Linda and those books, I learned how to differentiate between an adjective, an adverb, and a regular verb!

I also believe Linda was the one who taught me how to see women as equals. She's a couple of years older than me, and as children we had as much fun doing those Mad Libs as we did exploring an old farmhouse in the field behind her home or playing with her dolls and plastic horses. There wasn't "girl fun" and "boy fun." Linda just showed me that fun was fun, and there were many ways to find it. We just had fun together, and I had a great deal of respect for her.

I guess you don't realize how important someone is to you or how much influence they've had on who you've become until you really stop along your journey and reflect.

When the authorities arrested Jesus, his disciples scattered and hid. Peter, however, discreetly followed Jesus to the courtyard where the Sanhedrin court charged Jesus with his crimes. A few people identified Peter as one of Jesus's disciples, but Peter denied the accusation. After three years of traveling with Jesus, listening to his teachings, learning from him, eating with him both sacred and ordinary meals, sleeping along the roadways and in homes with him, and seeing the miracles he'd manifested, in this critical moment the disciples lost faith in Jesus's power and ran away.

It was just a short time before all this that Jesus questioned them about who they believed he was. Peter, with the assent of the rest, I'm sure, professed Jesus as the Son of God, the Messiah. Yet we must wonder what this actually meant to them when they failed to stick around when things got really tough.

However, let's jump ahead a couple of weeks. It was the Feast of Pentecost, and Jesus was no longer physically among them. A great many people were in Jerusalem for the feast and we soon found the disciples out in the public eye and preaching to people about Jesus, the Messiah sent by God. What changed in that group of fearful and scattered friends of Jesus to this now bold and united group of preachers? What occurred during the interlude?

The gospels all concur about the crucified Jesus returning from the dead and appearing to them in his resurrected form. We also learn that Jesus spent time with them explaining why everything happened as it did. And the climactic moment preceding the Pentecost preaching is the indwelling of the Holy Spirit upon this group. We can lump all this together into one phrase: *pause and reflect.*

The gospels are silent about the day *after* the crucifixion. It's the Sabbath, and every Jew is required to observe it. We can only assume that the disciples were simply keeping a very low profile in Jerusalem as they feared for their lives. We know that they'd somehow come back together. What have they been doing in this time? Most likely, they've been reflecting on how this ending has broken the dreams they had adopted from Jesus's teachings. The future they envisioned was gone. The finality of the dream had ended abruptly and violently. They were in shock and, more than likely, the denial stage of grief that Elisabeth Kübler-Ross described in her book *On Death and Dying.*[19]

In this denial stage, the reality of the event is too great to accept all at once. The person is running through various alternative options with preferable outcomes: "Jesus did not die. He has somehow fooled everyone. That battered body wasn't Jesus. It had to be someone else." The disciples are more than likely running through such scenarios in their minds because the

---

[19] Kübler-Ross, E., *On Death and Dying*, Routledge, 1969.

enormity of their loss is simply too great to grasp at this moment. And that means they're less than likely reflecting on any future plans or goals right now in their grief. To process through their grief in a natural way will take months or longer.

Yet something changes. In a matter of weeks, they become bold and daring, willing to risk their lives to tell people they're followers of Jesus, the executed criminal who bore the identity as God's Anointed One.

What changed for them? The obvious answer for many is that they experienced the presence of Jesus resurrected from the dead. From the moment Jesus appears to his disciples in the flesh following his devastating torture and death, something begins to stir in the disciples to strengthen their resolve and encourage their faith. The book of the Acts of the Apostles written by Luke shares that Jesus invested another forty days of instruction in them before he left them again. It can be inferred that Jesus went over many of his teachings once more now that they had a completely new revelation of who Jesus really was. Luke then tells us that the disciples, including the many women who followed, spent a great deal of time together in prayer and fellowship (see Acts 1:14), a time we can surely understand involved time for pause and reflection.

During this period, they came to appreciate the person of Jesus more than they'd understood during those days before the crucifixion. It was now in his absence that they understood the power of his presence. Only now did they fully appreciate the depth of his teachings and the transforming power of his lifestyle of grace and mercy that was the form of God's love in this world.

When I was nineteen years old, I lost a friend to cancer when she was only twenty years of age. She'd battled it for more than a year, but it was pretty aggressive. It wasn't until some months after she'd died that the depth of her friendship truly impacted me. It was in a moment in which I heard a song by an artist she'd constantly tried to get me to listen to that I truly recognized her life's importance and impact upon me. I broke down and cried, realizing how much I had taken for granted and not understood until I now realized her absence was final.

NOW CONSIDER THIS

These moments at the end of each chapter are exactly what this chapter is focusing on: pause and reflect. How would your life be fuller if you intentionally paused and reflected each night on your day and appreciated the people, events, and discoveries that day had brought you?

CHAPTER 5

Thank God for the Radicals

Some people live life by their own rules, preferring to draw outside the lines, think outside the box, and park in their own imaginary spaces. While this may aggravate those who want to follow the rules and have order, progress demands that some of us push those lines.

My friend and I decided one day to be "radical"
by parking against the lines in the church lot.

Some very famous people are known today precisely because they went outside the known lines of life and reached for something new.

Louis Pasteur developed the theory of germs when others believed there weren't things too small to be seen. Thanks to him we live longer and healthier lives.

Werner Heisenberg developed the foundational theory for quantum mechanics that became the basis for the computer.

Voltaire, the French writer, championed the concepts of free trade, civil liberties, and freedom of religion.

English filmmaker, Alfred Hitchcock, broke all the rules and even killed off the star in one of his movies in the first twenty-five minutes!!

Marie Curie was the first women to receive the Nobel Prize and the first person to win it for two separate categories. Her first award was for research into radioactivity (physics, 1903). Her second Nobel Prize was for chemistry in 1911. A few years later, she also helped develop the first X-ray machines!

These and many others in history were folks who didn't live by the status quo. They looked at life differently, from various angles, and developed the ideas and technology that moved us forward in our growth.

Often, they were persecuted for their thinking. People reacted to their ideas as radical, dangerous, and worthy of execution. However, once the ideas took over, and life progressed, people became grateful for their courage in leading us forward. From martyrs to saints, from persecuted to heroes, we now praise those we once despised and rejected.

Jesus of Nazareth fits into this list as an innovator as well. For many people then, as well as a great many today, God is perceived as an angry judge. God is like a cosmic Santa Claus bestowing gifts upon the good and righteous while delivering the proverbial coal, burning fiercely as it's plucked straight from the eternal fires of hell for the naughty and unrighteous ones. Jesus's teachings about God were advanced for the people of his time. He brought God from the high and lofty realm of heaven down to the earth where God was to be experienced as a kind, loving, and merciful father. Jesus's God was not so much an intimidating and inaccessible deity removed from the suffering and challenging life events of the people as he was a father in relationship with the people on a daily basis. It's difficult to recognize the power this alternative way of seeing God had on society then. Yet this simple teaching threatened to unravel the foundation of their society from its religious establishment to its financial institutions. Let me explain.

In Jesus's time, the social, financial, and religious aspects of society were all intertwined like a rope. Anything done to disrupt one aspect unraveled the whole of society. The religious way of life dictated the way people earned a living, how they spent their income, how they were taxed on it, how they fit in socially in their communities, and how they were connected to God as well.

As an example, a man born into a family of skilled carpenters, as Jesus was, was then expected to be a carpenter himself, especially as the oldest son. This was the societal expectation and was firmly backed by their understanding of God and the religious teachings they followed. He was expected to live by the rules, both written and unwritten, in his society. This would bring continued honor to the family and the family name. Honor brought work to the family business. Honor brought standing in the community that gave the family a religious stature. Honor was a sign of God's blessing upon the family. If the son dishonored it, and brought shame upon himself, it brought shame upon his whole family. The family business would be shunned by the community. The family would be rejected from the worshiping community. Financial ruin then brought hunger, homelessness, and isolation. The consequences were tragic, and God's punishment was deemed justly fulfilled. To save a remnant of the family from such shame, the offender would either be removed from the public eye (locked up, as it were, within the family home) or face shunning (still observed in Amish communities in my area of Pennsylvania), exiled, or if truly abhorrent, put to death publicly as an "honor killing." In many Middle Eastern countries today, "honor killing" is practiced on the daughters who are sexually assaulted or have consensual sex (the difference does not matter as the "shame" is the daughter is no longer a virgin), and for various other matters deemed to bring shame upon the family.

Knowing this cultural mindset, it makes a much more powerful story of Jesus standing up for the woman caught in adultery.[20]

It's kind of ironic that today many of those claiming to follow the Way of Jesus seem to come across more like the Pharisees and scribes who opposed him. They espouse judgment and condemnation against those who are different when Jesus embraced them and welcomed them into his new family. Strange, but not really unusual. Once a radical's ideas are accepted, a system rises up to codify the teachings, "boxing them in" so there can be no deviation of thought. A priestly class of persons are then set up as keepers of the "truth," and their role is to maintain order through conformity.

---

[20] See John 8:1–11

The God Path that Jesus walks is a radical departure from the one that the many follow. The "rules" are not as clearly defined that one can put them down in writing and then follow them. Jesus's foundation for the rules he followed was made of compassion, understanding, and focused on saving a life. This God Path is ever moving, ever adjusting to the situation and person. This God Path is followed by radicals. This God Path is about opening the path to the ones who've failed on the codified path of the institution.

NOW CONSIDER THIS

What "radical" belief have you felt God is affirming that breaks with the tradition you've been living under? What consequences would you face if you trusted in it? Would Life be the result for you and others?

CHAPTER 6

HAPPY TODAY!

"What day is it?" asked Pooh
"It's today!" squeaked Piglet.
"My favorite day," said Pooh.

A. A. Milne's stories of Winnie the Pooh give to us such beautiful words of wisdom in such simple exchanges between the characters. In those simple lines is a gift to all of us: a gift of peace, of focus, even of love and friendship.

Too often we have our attention focused on regrets and frustrations in the past or anxiety about our future.

We dread Mondays, tolerate Tuesdays, begin to have hope on Wednesdays, suffer through Thursdays, revel in Fridays, and fill up Saturdays and Sundays with activity. And then we start it all over again.

Imagine that no matter what day it is when you wake up, you said to yourself and those you encounter, "Happy today!"

I started doing this recently, and it had a profound impact on my perception and ultimately, on my life. By saying this to myself and to others, I revealed within myself a view of life as precious and important. The day became a precious moment in time that I had been gifted by God. I celebrated the people I encountered that day because this was the day God had given me to be with them. Life has become a joy each day because I am not looking at tomorrow or yesterday. I'm working on being totally present in today.

The psalmist declared that *this* is the day that God made; and we need to celebrate *it* and find joy in *this day!*[21]

Jesus said, "Repent, for the kingdom of God is at hand."[22] It's here, now, in your midst! He then said to "seek first the kingdom of God."[23] How? How do you seek this kingdom that seems invisible to our eyes? By opening your eyes and your heart to *this* day—today! Expect to see God revealing His presence everywhere throughout your day!

Jesus also said to pray, "Give us *this day* our *daily* bread."[24] While bread was the staple of the people's diet in their culture, bread can also be taken as a call to us to seek Jesus, the bread of life, *each* day in the day we are living—*today!*

May *today* be your favorite day—every day!

NOW CONSIDER THIS

The God Path is not a physical trail as much as it is a trail of perspective and vision from the heart. To see it with your mind's eye, you must submit to its spiritual reality. Right now, say to yourself, "Happy today!" Say it again, just loud enough for you to hear it as you look around at the world you are in right at this moment. What do you see? If you could hear the thoughts of others around you right now, what would they be saying to themselves? How might they benefit from proclaiming this a happy day?

---

21 See Psalm 118:24
22 Matthew 3:2, NASB
23 Matthew 6:33, NASB
24 Matthew 6:11, NASB

CHAPTER 7

LIVING THE DREAM—GOD'S WAY!

> Am I living the 'just get by' plan, or is there a greater God-dream that, if lived to the fullest, could permeate and inform every move I make?
>
> —Michael Slaughter, *Dare to Dream*

The Rev. Michael Slaughter is pastor of the Ginghamsburg UMC in Ohio where he went in 1979 to a congregation of ninety in the middle of nowhere and, through trusting in God's dream for him and the congregation, grew the congregation over the past thirty-five years to about four thousand members. Ginghamsburg Church is a multisite megachurch located in Tipp City, Ohio, a suburb thirteen miles north of Dayton, Ohio. It hosts nearly five thousand people of all ages on its three campuses each week at the ten different worship services. It's currently the fourth-largest United Methodist church in the United States. It has repeatedly been named one of the most influential churches in America.

Rev. Slaughter challenges the readers of his book *Dare to Dream: Creating a God-Sized Mission Statement for Your Life* to ask themselves this question for themselves: "Am I living the 'just get by' plan, or is there a greater God-dream that, if lived to the fullest, could permeate and inform every move I make?"

I asked myself this question and prayed about it. Believing that there was a God Path that I was made to walk, I leaned into God's heart through prayer and reflection, asking what this God dream might be. Over the years I have continued to come back to one overreaching concept:

love. I've been made in the image of God (love), and I'm fulfilling my God dream when I surrender completely into being love.

When I choose love as my response to anything in life, it can be an easy step, or it can be a very difficult step, but the moment I choose love, I feel like I've come home to myself. It's in this moment that I choose to be who I am and to live out from the essence of who I am in the depths of my being. Anything else is in conflict with my inner core, my essential nature and identity, and leads me into tension and stress.

To act out of who I am is freeing. Yet for many of us, we've lost this ability. Perhaps it was disciplined out of us as children. In an effort to teach us to be compassionate and care about others, the lesson to care about ourselves was neglected. We became more concerned about what others felt than our own feelings, more troubled by how others might think of us than what we thought about ourselves. And in the process we became ensnared in a web of anxiety trying to please everyone at the expense of caring for ourselves. This is not love. This is fear. This is living from a fear-based life in which we act out of the dread of what others may think about us. It's disguised as "sacrificial love," and we imagine ourselves as a martyr. However, it is not truly living out of God's love from which we were formed. It's a distortion.

For most of my ministry, I've lived out of such a distorted love. Playing the role of a pastor, I've sacrificed time with my wife and children to be at the beck and call of my congregation. I'd attend every meeting, be at every hospital bed, visit the homebound, have an open door so whenever someone dropped in at the church, they could come in and talk with me. I often worked into the late hours of the night and into the early morning hours to get sermons completed, paperwork finished, reports filled out, and special projects concluded. I did this believing I was acting from my love for the people, the ministry, for even God! However, most of it was accomplished out of a fear within that I would be rejected or that others would think less of me, or that I might lose my job.

Now, listen. I'm *not* saying that these things weren't important or that they didn't need to be done. No, they're important, and they do need to be done with care. What I'm saying is that I was motivated by a false understanding of love. It was fear disguised as love. I was fooling myself into believing I was responding from love within me to expressing love, but I was actually expressing love from a place of fear. Does this make sense to you? If so, you're probably asking, "How do we fix this?"

It starts with awareness, so if you're now aware of this tendency in you, you've made a huge step forward. Then it takes prayer. Sharing this fear with God and allowing God to shine light ever deeper into your heart is how we begin cleaning out the basement of our lives of all the hidden and forgotten stuff that made us fearful in the first place. For this exercise, I also recommend you find a trusted friend or spiritual counselor to help you dig this stuff out and find a healthy way to deal with it. Finally, you'll begin the work of consciously focusing on the natural and foundational love that formed you. As time goes on, you'll need to be less and less conscious of doing it, and more and more, it will become your natural response. John Wesley, the founder of the Methodist movement, believed in the perfecting of love that's stated in the first biblical letter of John:

> By this love is perfected with us, so that we may have confidence for the Day of Judgment, because as he is so also are we in this world. There is no fear in love, but perfect love casts out fear.[25]

John Wesley understood that the biblical use of the words *perfect* and *perfection* weren't to be taken in the moral sense. He didn't believe it was possible that human beings could reach a state of flawlessness or faultlessness. *Perfection* would be better understood as "completeness" or even "wholeness". Wesley believed that in Christ our sin is removed and we're thus made whole or complete in love. Love then would become the source of our actions and words.

So let's return to the question with which Mike Slaughter challenged us: "Am I living the 'just get by' plan, or is there a greater God-dream that, if lived to the fullest, could permeate and inform every move I make?"

The God dream is manifested in you and me. We're all God's dream made real. Instilled in us from the beginning of creation is that very image of God: divine and true love. To embrace that truth is to embrace the potential of a life lived without fear. Are you willing? Are you ready?

NOW CONSIDER THIS

Start with one area in your life that you now realize is a place that you live out from fear. Is it in your work? Is it in your family? Is it with your friends? Choose one thing where fear of consequences is the reason you respond the way you do. Now look at how you can respond completely from love in that situation. Ask yourself the powerful question: What would Jesus do?

---

[25] 1 John 4:17–18. ESV

CHAPTER 8

EMBRACING OUR VULNERABILITY!

Thanksgiving 2015 was different than the past fifty-four Thanksgivings I had enjoyed in my life. This was the first one in which my dad was not with his family at the dinner table. On September 23, he succumbed to a ten-year battle with Alzheimer's, heart issues, and cancer.

This had me contemplating the stages of life and the changes that are inevitable. As I remarked to a high school friend whose mother is nearing the end of her earthly journey, we're now at that age where we're losing our parents and our children are becoming more independent. For a time, our children needed us. Then both our children and our parents needed us. Then, neither need us, and we're suddenly wondering, "What do we do now?"

In some ways, this becomes an age of vulnerability. I believe we're probably vulnerable our whole lives in some sense, but throughout most of our younger years we live in the illusion we're invincible and immortal. We take risks that are often dangerous in those early years because we don't have an awareness of our mortality. Abusing our bodies with drugs, alcohol, excessive amounts of junk food, driving too fast, and many other physical feats that threaten our very existence are part of our youthful indiscretions. We feel invincible. We believe we're invulnerable. Any hint of vulnerability is a negative emotion that we challenge by doing something to prove our fearlessness. But is vulnerability really a terrible thing? As we reach middle age, we begin to become aware that life is passing by, and we only have a finite time in this world. Can accepting our vulnerability become a strong position from which to live?

I believe the answer is yes. I believe that accepting our vulnerability can essentially become a freeing and empowering position in which to live. Author Brené Brown has written a terrific book on vulnerability, *Daring Greatly*, which takes its title from a speech President Theodore Roosevelt gave at the Sorbonne in Paris, France, on April 23, 1910. This passage from that speech made it famous:

> It is not the critic who counts; not the man who points out how the strong man stumbles, or where the doers of deeds could have done better.
>
> The credit belongs to the man who is actually in the arena, whose face is marred by dust and sweat and blood; who strives valiantly; who errs, who comes up short again and again,
>
> Because there is no effort without error and shortcoming; but who does actually strive to do the deeds; who knows great enthusiasms, the great devotions; who spends himself in a worthy cause;
>
> Who at the best knows in the end the triumph of high achievement, and who at the worst, if he fails, at least fails while daring greatly.

To dare greatly is to risk failing, which is to open oneself to being vulnerable to attacks from others as well as from within oneself. Within ourselves, we may feel inadequate, and the immature person will respond in one of two ways. Either this person will take a risk that has little payoff except to bolster the individual's ego, or this one will retreat from any action out of fear of failure. However, the mature person responds to feelings of inadequacy by advancing forward in a quest to achieve a victory over self *and* for the betterment of others.

In a very literal sense of this are the actions of young men and women in combat situations. A friend of mine, Tom, shared very reluctantly his experience in Vietnam. In the jungle, he and his fellow soldiers were under heavy attack. His friend was next to him when a mortar went off right by them as they were down low and back to back to protect one another. Suddenly, they were knocked to the ground by an explosion. Tom was able to roll over and checked on his buddy. Only the top half of his buddy was there. The fear Tom had increased as he saw how fragile life, his life, truly was. He could've become paralyzed by that fear. Yet his training and maturity caused his response to be one of action. He kept up the fight. He was fighting for his life as well as his other brothers in arms. He wanted them all to survive.

This is what our embracement of our vulnerability can help us accomplish when we find ourselves in some arena or jungle of fear. It isn't a guarantee of success, but to not act is certain failure. To act is to "dare greatly."

Jesus dared his disciples to follow his lead and take on the fake leaders of the day. He called out King Herod (Jesus called him "that fox," which was a very derogatory and treasonous statement), the Pharisees (he called them "whitewashed tombs" because they were concerned more about how others perceived them than they were about their own souls), and the scribes (the legal experts on Scripture who managed to find ways to lay heavy burdens of the Law on the poor people that kept them enslaved and without hope). Jesus called out their hypocrisy, which everyone saw, but would not speak out loud for fear of losing their lives. The God Path is not all sunshine and rainbows. It can, at times, be fraught with danger.

NOW CONSIDER THIS

What is your usual response to a dangerous situation where your job or a relationship or a comfortable place may be in jeopardy if you were to risk speaking up about a wrong or an injustice? Is it to do nothing? Do you try to ignore it and hope it just clears up on its own? Or do you risk those things and find a way to speak up for what you believe is right and just? What would it take for you to have the courage to dare greatly?

CHAPTER 9

FIND YOUR BIG WHY

Tom Stephens is a great salesman, one of those highly motivated individuals who succeeds a large percentage of the time. It's because he heard one of the greatest motivational speeches of his life one night having dinner with his wife. As they ate, she reached across the table and put her hand on his and said, "Honey, I'm pregnant." Those three words instantly motivated him to do better because now he had a bigger why to succeed.[26]

Randy Leamer had a young daughter who was going to die if she didn't receive a new kidney. Randy wanted to give his kidney, but the doctors refused to let him because he was so overweight. But they gave him eight months to lose 100 pounds. He lost the weight and said it wasn't really that difficult to do. Why? Because he had a great incentive—to save his daughter's life![27] He had his bigger why to keep him focused.

> If you have a big enough why, you'll always discover the how.

As your why gets bigger, you stop holding back and start going all out. When I was seventeen, I began to feel a call from God to explore the ordained ministry. I had grown up in the church and enjoyed my life there. I enjoyed the youth groups, the youth choir I participated in, the various church plays that I acted and sang in, and then one day while listening to the pastor preaching,

[26] http://www.jonisjems.com/uploads/2/6/4/3/26430872/yourwhy.pdf.
[27] Ibid.

I suddenly had this thought come to me that I could do that. It was strange to me because my real goal was to go to college and become a teacher. I was a youth, and working with children and youth was where I found myself most comfortable. However, I figured that this might be something I should at least consider.

As some time went on and I felt more of a tug upon my heart, I made an appointment with my pastor to talk about this feeling. With his blessing and advice, I began my journey and met with our congregation's staff-parish relations committee, which had the task of being the first to explore my calling. They approved, and at the next annual Charge Conference with the district superintendent officiating, I was brought up for a vote to the larger administrative body of the church. After their approval, I was then handed off to the District Committee on Ordained Ministry (dCOM) who would then work with me through the long process of discerning my gifts and graces and fulfilling our United Methodist denomination's process toward ordination. I was under this group's oversight for six to seven years while attending college part-time and working full-time as a school bus driver. In my senior year, with just four months to go until graduation, I found myself doubting my calling.

My original desire to be a school teacher was being fanned by the daily interactions I was having with the children and youth on my school bus. Some of these kids I watched grow from middle school through high school and then graduate while I was on this same route for the several years I drove the bus. Additionally, I was enjoying the learning process I was in at the college level, and I admired many of my professors.

So I made a decision. I'd drop out of the ministry process and do whatever it took to become a schoolteacher. First, I went to the department head of my major at Trenton State College, Robert Anderson, and explained my desire. He was concerned. I was about to graduate and would be starting all over. Then he had an idea: stay in my degree program, graduate, then apply to the master's program and earn a teaching certificate at the same time. It would save me time and potentially give me a higher status and pay scale when I completed my master's! This sounded good to me and so that became my plan. I informed my family and my church, along with the dCOM that I was heading in a new direction. My heart was light, and I was excited!

Now I'd been listening to a specific Christian radio program for a few years and continued to do so. This program was done live most of the time and featured call-in times where listeners called in and shared their struggles, their joys, and their questions with the host, Rev. Wayne Monbleau. I would listen in my car or bus as I drove during his show. So many callers would share their fears that they had failed God, that God was angry with them, or that the church they had attended had judged them unworthy of membership. As the next few months passed by, I found myself aching for these people who'd been hurt by pastors and churches whose "God" permitted them to dismiss others. Their God was an angry judge who seemed to hate humanity so much that this God's son, Jesus, had apparently come to earth to appease his father's bloodthirst by being crucified. However, the God I had come to know was through the loving grace with which Jesus preached. One day, I was alone in my school bus, hearing another child of God sharing their pain inflicted on them by another misguided preacher/teacher, and I cried out to God. "Why, God, do you let these people into ministry? Why do you let them hurt your children like this!" I could almost see God in my mind's eye, or maybe my heart's eye, slowly shaking His head and grieving. And then I felt God's message to me: "Tom, that's why I called you into ministry. I need you and others who know me to bring healing to my hurting children."

The next week, I made an appointment with my pastor and told him I wanted to return to the ordained ministry process. I had to answer a lot of questions from the dCOM when I met again with them, but it was worth it. I now had my why for the ministry.

To truly *get* motivated, the first thing you have to do is to discover what the big *why* is. I had found my big *why*. See how it makes a difference in the following illustration:

One day a journalist happened upon a worksite. She noticed three bricklayers and asked each of them what they were doing.

The first one, whom she noticed was working very apathetically, replied, "Whaddaya think I'm doin'? I'm layin' brick!"

The second bricklayer, who was a bit more involved in the work, said, "I'm building a wall."

But the third bricklayer, who was totally absorbed in the work, replied, "I'm building a cathedral for the Lord!"[28]

To *stay* motivated, you must continuously keep reminding yourself of your why.

And Tom Stephens? Well, his wife helped him stay motivated by giving him two more whys.

---

[28] Ibid.

NOW CONSIDER THIS

In your present life situation, are you more like the first bricklayer, the second, or the third? Do you have a sense of the *big* picture of what you're doing in your life as it fits in with God's master plan to connect people everywhere into his kingdom? Take a few moments to pray and then write out your *why* here.

CHAPTER 10

THE BIG TEMPTATION TO QUIT

"What are you giving up for Lent?" I remember hearing this question from my friends when I was a child. Some of us gave up chocolate. Others gave up other candy and things that we loved. Lent was considered a time to make yourself suffer as we saw it. And I didn't quite understand the reasoning behind it. After all, Jesus had died on a cross nearly two thousand years ago to save us. Why should we now punish ourselves for forty days when we were forgiven?

The reality is that the church set aside these forty days before Easter Sunday to seek some time in prayer and reflection for the mysterious gift God had bestowed upon humanity through His Son, Jesus. It was supposed to be a time of prayer, and the tradition of giving something up was to be a continual reminder of our call to prayer. One way that I decided to use this time many years ago was to put my watch on my right wrist. Every time I looked at my left wrist to see what time it was, I was forced to remember that my watch was on the other arm to call me into a time of prayer.

Lent is also supposed to be a time that we seek God in prayer to allow God to transform us. I'd like to take you to a Scripture verse where Jesus is dealing with his own forty days of struggle. In particular, In Matthew 4:8–9, Jesus is taken up to a very high mountain where he is shown a great and vast lay of the world and all its kingdoms. The tempter offers Jesus everything he sees for one simple thing in return: Jesus just needs to go to his knees and put his face to the ground and ascribe to the tempter his worth as Jesus's leader.

What is the temptation here for Jesus? In one way, he's being given the opportunity to assume the role presently held by the Roman emperor.

In another way, this is actually a temptation for Jesus to accept the status quo, to give up any attempt to change things, to heal the brokenness, to empower people through a transformative understanding of God. The tempter is saying to Jesus, "Just acknowledge that selfishness prevails, Jesus, and rule as everyone else does. Don't waste your time and energy trying to show people they can change. They can't! They won't! Just *fit in* with us, Jesus, and you'll live a much happier life."

As a pastor, I find this temptation is strong in the church. Congregations want to be lively and vital. They want to have worship that lifts them up and encourages them. They want to see their pews or chairs filled on Sunday mornings. Yet the tempter is whispering in our ears. When someone says we should do something that's going to require more time, money, and people to make a difference, the tempter whispers, "We don't have that kind of money," or, "It'll be the same few people who will do all the work." Jesus faced this often in his ministry.

In the sixth chapter of Mark's gospel, Mark tells of a time in Jesus's ministry when the great crowd that had been following him had stayed with Jesus into the later evening hours. The disciples were weary and suspected as much with Jesus. They needed a break. They went to Jesus and pointed out the obvious: it's late and we're far from any village and people need to eat. It's time to send these people off. It had been a long day that started with Jesus attempting to take his disciples to a deserted place for some rest! The disciples were at least polite about it and told Jesus that the people probably were hungry, and they should go and find a village and seek food.

Here, we see on the surface what looks like an expression of compassion for the people by the disciples. They recognize the lateness of the hour, the possibility of the people's hunger, and that they may need to start seeking a place to bed down for the night. However, Jesus doesn't allow them to shrug off their own potential to do something. He retorts, "*You* give them something to eat." This is completely unexpected. I can imagine the looks on their faces as they're taken aback, crying, "*What? Us?* Where are we going to get enough money to buy all these people food?!"

This is the challenging thing about Jesus. He isn't content with the status quo, of how things have always been or how things are always perceived. He believes in a far greater power to transform people from accepting one type of reality to living into a far more powerful one. The disciples push back. They see a problem from an accepted angle and only one possible solution. The tempter is whispering in their ears: "This would cost two hundred days' wages! Jesus can't be serious! Be realistic!"

It's not inconceivable that the disciples may be hitting another obstacle to following Jesus at this point. The temptation to quit and go back to a life that makes sense, no matter how difficult it may be, must be pulling at their spirits. Jesus most assuredly senses their frustration and the lure of walking away, and so he gives them a simple task to do—a first step that is believable:

Jesus challenges them by asking them to settle down and take stock first. "How much do you have on hand?" he asks. "Go and look and tell me what we have," he continues. They come up with five loaves of bread and a couple of smoked fish.

The total of five loaves of bread and two fish will be a confirmation to the disciples that they are just not prepared to fulfill Jesus's command. Maybe now Jesus will agree with them. But remember at the start of this chapter Jesus faced a temptation to accept the status quo and to rule the way kings and emperors had ruled. He rejected it.

Jesus rejected the tempter's view of life and recited the truth from Deuteronomy 6:13 that it is complete trust in God that offers the only power to live a life of full potential and possibility.

Many times in life you will feel the temptation to quit when things get really difficult. Your dream, your vision, will be seemingly crushed by others, and a whisper will run through your mind to just accept what is and what it must be. But men and women of ordinary talents and extraordinary dreams rejected the status quo that creates injustice and inequality and oppression. Their names are legendary to us: Mahatma Gandhi, Mother Teresa, Martin Luther King Jr., Abraham Lincoln, Amelia Earhart, Susan B. Anthony, Harriet Tubman, and many, many more.

Don't accept that things are unchangeable. Don't give in to the temptation to just fit in and allow hopelessness and defeat to overwhelm you. We worship a God who believes in us.

NOW CONSIDER THIS

The late NFL head coach George Allen was quoted as saying the following about not quitting:

> People of mediocre ability sometimes achieve outstanding success because they don't know when to quit. Most men succeed because they are determined to.[29]

---

[29] https://www.brainyquote.com/quotes/george_allen_sr_377151

What thing do you believe in so much but are feeling beaten down to the point a "voice" within is tempting you to give up and quit? Do you care enough to keep on going with a determination to do all you can, no matter how far you may have to go? I recommend watching the video "Rocky's Inspirational Speech to his Son" from the 2006 movie *Rocky Balboa* on YouTube. Truly inspiring.

CHAPTER 11

WHO CARES?

Who cares? When you hear that question, it can mean "I'm doing what I want to do no matter what you think." I remember saying this in that manner to my mom as a teenager. However, it can also mean "No one seems to really care about me." It's a question of near hopelessness. Yet it seems to be raising the slightest glimmer of hope asking if there is anyone who does care.

I believe we all have days where we feel like no one seems to care. Life is hard and sometimes beats down the best of us. Jesus even seemed to have days like this. Those feelings may have been lurking behind his question of his disciples when he asked them,

> Who do people say that the Son of Man is? (Matthew 16:13, ESV)

This is followed by,

> But who do you say that I am? (Matthew 16:15, ESV)

Later, when large numbers turned away from him, Jesus turned to his disciples and asked,

> Do you also wish to go away? (John 6:67, ESV)

Then there is that moment in the garden of Gethsemane. When he returns from praying for strength for the impending death he faces, he finds his friends asleep and asks:

Could you not stay awake with me one hour? (Matthew 26:40, ESV)

And perhaps no more poignant than in his final words on the cross, there was that horrible sense of being abandoned and that no one seemed to care, not even God:

My God, my God, why have You forsaken me? (Matthew 27:46, ESV)

Jesus is well acquainted with that feeling of loneliness and despair. While he most certainly loved and enjoyed the friendship he had with the disciples, his mission was a difficult one and brought many instances of frustration and doubts.

Yet he persevered. He never saw the obstacles as insurmountable. They were merely hurdles he had to overcome to remain faithful to his Father's calling.

You and I experience this on our own God Path as well. My calling into ministry was so strong and palatable when I was younger. I thought I would feel that presence of God for the rest of my life. Yet here I am forty years later and find myself at times feeling alone. People attack me at times, thinking they are following their own call from God to critique me, but it comes over much more like criticism. I can find myself caught in between two lovers: my wife and my ministry in the church. Each has a valid call upon my life, and yet I can find myself not able to give each the time they deserve. Who cares? I wonder. The answer then comes to me—they all care. They all care about me and what I'm doing. They all care about my health—my spiritual, physical, and emotional health. However, it isn't up to them to give up their needs for me for the sake of the other. It is up to me to create balance in both my personal and public lives.

To do this, I must become less reactive and more proactive. I must better prepare my schedule for attending to all the needs before me in a proactive way. I must resist reacting to every demand, every single need no matter the size or significance. Obviously there are emergencies that arise and must be attended to within a timely manner. But we've all been derailed by the less significant need that is overblown by some as a major crisis. It is up to us to be prepared by discerning the true level of need. Because ultimately, the answer to who cares needs to be found within. I care about myself. And God cares enough to let you discover that and follow that goal for balance to achieve it.

NOW CONSIDER THIS

Think of a time where you felt alone and maybe even abandoned by God and family. What made you feel this way?

    What did you do that made things worse for you?

    What did you do that was helpful?

    What can you do to be better prepared for the next time? (Yes, there will be a next time.)

CHAPTER 12

ANGRY OR AFRAID?

Let's be honest—people are very afraid in this day and age. And fear really messes with our minds. When churches, families, or nations act out of fear, they often move in ways that are *contrary* to the Spirit of God. A prime example is the way our politicians have used fear to manipulate people over the years. They make us fear the other party, fear people of other religions, fear other countries, and ultimately, to fear each other.

One agitator of fear is change. Things are changing at a high rate of speed, and as we experience these changes, many of us are scratching our heads and falling behind. Technology is advancing so fast that even our youth may not able to keep up at times! Now *that's fast!*

And all these changes incite more fears. As Kim Shockley, the coauthor of *The Surprise Factor*, notes so well, "We are afraid of hurting someone's feelings, we are afraid of financial institutions, or we are afraid that someone will leave our church or that the 'wrong' people will start attending. We are afraid we will do the wrong thing or fail doing the right thing. We are afraid that we will upset the power people or the money people ... the list goes on and on."[30]

---

[30] Nixon, Paul and Kim Shockley, *The Surprise Factor: Gospel Strategies for Changing the Game at Your Church*, Abingdon Press, 2013.

> Some of the worst fights I have seen at church are related to human attempts to try and freeze changes that scare us.
> —Paul Nixon, coauthor of *The Surprise Factor*

With all these things frightening us, we look for a place where we can feel secure, a place where life is familiar and doesn't change. We want some control over our lives. The church becomes that place where we seek such a static environment. Yet, the church may be the one place that should be *leading* change. Jesus tells a woman that God is seeking people who will worship in spirit and truth (John 4:23), not in a temple or on a certain mountain. Jesus informs a religious scholar that those who are true worshipers of God will be like the wind, ever-changing and moving and uncontainable (John 3:5-8).

No wonder the church experiences such unrest!

Somehow, when we read these verses today, we tame the wildness out of them and make Christianity something motionless, lifeless, and dead. Jesus says, "Take up your cross and follow me," and we turn his words into, "Place a nice brass cross on an altar and sit still and don't rock the boat." Jesus calls us to an adventure, and we want to sit in God's living room and just watch the slide show of others who have gone on the trip!

Now, I'm not saying that taking Jesus at his word isn't scary. I too am frightened by the call God lays upon us as a church community. Shockley notes that "fear is normal, but when it takes over, it is a sign that we need to get *re-centered spiritually as a community.*"[31]

In one church where I had been serving for over a decade, the leadership agreed to re-center the church meetings. We agreed to make all our meetings more spirit centered. We spent time not only praying, but studying together, challenging one another to become aware of God's presence and work in our lives, and sharing the movement of the Holy Spirit in our lives personally and in the church.

And we prayerfully, and not without a little anxiousness, chose to be bold and follow the Spirit's leading. We were met with some who rejoiced and some who did not rejoice. It's challenging trying to follow the Spirit, but we determined to be more afraid of extinguishing the Spirit than in pleasing everyone (which we all know is not very likely).

---

[31] Ibid.

What happened was golden. We grew closer together as leaders and more supportive of one another. We brought all our ministries into focus toward the same God-inspired goals. The empowering of God's Spirit was exciting! It was transforming and strengthening to each of us.

NOW CONSIDER THIS

A good question to ask ourselves and pray about when we are afraid is "What am I *really* afraid of?" The answer will set you free from fear.

CHAPTER 13

PERFECTION OR EXCELLENCE?

It's funny how you can completely forget something until, one day, something happens or someone says something that reignites an old memory.

In doing some preliminary research for a sermon series, I came across an idea that reminded me of my first-grade teacher, Miss Smithgall.

Miss Smithgall was about 150 years old and wore the same purple-and-blue dress every day and these slipper-type shoes. She was a no-nonsense teacher of first-graders who demanded the best of her students. She rewarded you with a single jellybean if you earned a 100 on a spelling test and struck fear into the hearts of her students with her strength of character, though she was a small, frail-looking woman.

I was a good student and earned my share of jellybeans (though I didn't like them at all back then and usually gave them to my friends). However, at times I felt awkward being singled out and took a little teasing from my friends. So, one day I was doing a coloring project, which I loved to do, and did not really do my best on it. Miss Smithgall knew it wasn't my normal coloring best, and she said to me, "Tommy, that's not your best. You can do better. Don't lower your standards to be like others. Let them raise theirs to be like yours."

I didn't quite understand all of what she was saying then, but I did know I'd let myself down by purposely doing poorly. From then on, I gave my best effort on everything.

I've learned that my best effort isn't about perfection but about excellence. We often confuse these two ideas as being synonymous, but they're opposites! Kay Sharpe writes in her Radical

Reformation blog[32] that "perfectionism is driven by a fear of failure and doesn't take risks. Excellence is a Kingdom character *trait* that is an expression of one's joy in the relationship we have with the Lord. It flows out of a grateful and generous heart."

Today, looking back on Miss Smithgall's admonition, I think I'd strive for excellence and take a risk. Maybe try coloring in an experimental way. After all, the renowned artists aimed for excellence in their art, not perfection that met how others set the standards. Maybe that's what Miss Smithgall was trying to tell that six-year old boy all those years ago.

NOW CONSIDER THIS

In this world, you're totally unique. There has never been another you before, and there'll never be another you again. For this time—for this place—you've been brought to life. You have an exclusive part to play in this world that no one else can fulfill. So rather than trying to conform to what everyone else is doing, why not let God direct you to your very own inimitable life?

In the words of Bill and Ted, what are ways that you can "be excellent"?[33]

---

[32] http://www.radical-reformation.org/2010/06/perfection-versus-excellence-there-is-a-difference/.

[33] Matheson, Chris and Ted Solomon, *Bill & Ted's Excellent Adventure*, produced by Interscope Communications and Nelson Entertainment, 1989.

CHAPTER 14

Giving It Your All

Serena and Venus Williams are well known in the tennis world and beyond. Venus tells the story about how her kid sister, Serena, helped her during a particularly grueling doubles match the two were playing one day. Venus's serves were terrible, and it was making their chance of winning very difficult. During a change of court where the players have a minute to sit and towel off, Serena said to Venus in a joking tone of voice, "Listen, I don't care what you do on your side of the court, but I'm not going to miss on my side. We will not lose this match."

Then Serena got serious. "Look, Venus, no matter how you feel about your game, you have to show up at the court, right? You're here to play tennis after all. But you *do* have a choice about whether you want to compete well or compete badly. I'm going to make the choice to compete well. Why don't you do that too?"[34]

Venus goes on to share how that simple advice was like a bright light went on inside her. "When you commit yourself to something, you can't find a way out of it. You can't say, 'Oh, I don't want to play today.' You have to go, and as long as you have to be there, why not give it your all? Why not give it the best you can? In other words, don't overlook the opportunity to achieve something, don't be nervous, don't hold back, give it all that you've got, because the moment may never come again."[35]

I think that's great advice for living life. We all face struggles in this world. Life isn't fair. Life isn't easy. But here we are. Now we didn't have the choice about being here, but we do have a

---

[34] Thomas, Marlo, and Friends, *The Right Words at the Right Time*, New York: Atria Publishing Group, 2002, 371–373.
[35] Ibid.

choice about how we are going to live. We can complain and whine about life's problems and our struggles, or we can choose to give this life we have our very best effort. Like Serena said about the tennis match, she could easily say to us about living life: "As long as you have to be here, why not give it your all? Why not give it the best you can?"

God has breathed into each of us the divine breath of life! Life for a glorious purpose! This is a great responsibility and an honor for us. Why would we dishonor God by allowing anything to distract us from that important task?

Let's not overlook the opportunity to achieve something. Let's not be nervous, or hold back, but give it all that we've got, because the moment may never come again.

NOW CONSIDER THIS

What's holding you back from giving it your all? Are you afraid you will fail? So what happens if you fail? More importantly, what happens if you succeed? This is your life, my friend. Show up for it and give it your all!!

CHAPTER 15

WIN OR LOSE?

The Olympics have ended as I write this. For two weeks this summer, the best athletes from around the world gathered to compete, to cheer one another on, and to build relationships between nations through the challenge and excitement of sports. Some people look at these events as an opportunity for each nation to make a statement about itself. Others watch for the thrill of seeing people who've given their lives to training for a moment in time. A moment in time where the world will see them give everything they've got for a few seconds, hoping that at the end of those few seconds, they'll be deemed the fastest, or strongest, or most talented, or simply the best in the entire world of seven billion people.

It amazes me that the difference between the gold and silver medal, the difference between being remembered and praised or forgotten, the difference between getting wealthy off endorsements or continuing to live a more challenging life, is sometimes a hundredth of a second! That's faster than the blink of an eye!! Imagine training for years and years, and in the race of your life, you swim or run faster than 6,999,999,998 of the people in the world! But one person goes a hundredth of a second faster. And that makes all the difference!!

I'm so thankful that this is not how God judges and rewards us. For God, it's not about winning or succeeding, but it's about taking part.

In the tenth chapter of Luke, Jesus appoints seventy persons to go out into the surrounding towns and places to deliver his message. He shares an image of the work that is ahead: "The harvest is plentiful, but the laborers are few."[36] He explains their mission and gives them authority to heal the sick.

---

[36] Luke 10:2 NRSV

Later, when they return to him, they are overjoyed at how even the demons submitted to them. And Jesus rejoices with them yet reminds them that they shouldn't rejoice in the power they had over demons, but that their "names are written in heaven" (Luke 10:20, NRSV). In other words, it's not what they accomplished, but that they were faithful in doing what they said they believed. This is what God rejoices in.

In 2013, Mary Shertenlieb was diagnosed with leukemia. This was her third time with a diagnosis of cancer. She began undergoing treatment and, in 2014, had a bone marrow transplant. She had never run the Boston Marathon before, but decided in 2018 to run it. She trained as intensely as she could and her doctors gave her permission to run it on one condition: if during the race at any time she felt sick, she should stop.

If you followed the race or heard any news about this race, you know it was a horrible day for the race. Temperatures hovered just above freezing, and rain fell throughout the day, at times in a downpour. Many seasoned runners fell short of their personal goals, some even dropping out.

Mary had made a decision to run for Dana-Farber to raise money for the cancer center that had helped her live again. Her shoes were already soaked through by the 11:15 a.m. start time. She wore a poncho with a hood to keep her chest from getting wet and cold because she was still taking immunosuppressants from the bone marrow transplant. But the wind would blow her hood back, and rain would pour down her back. She became soaked. At the halfway point, she decided to stop in briefly to the medical tent there. It was staffed by one of the nurses who had taken care of Mary in the cancer center. When she saw Mary, she was heartsick. Mary's lips were purple and her teeth were chattering uncontrollably. She implored Mary to sit and warm up for a while, but Mary felt she had to go on.

A few more miles down and Mary was now passing the five-hour mark for running. Most racers had completed the race. She was now running on the sidewalk because the roads had been reopened to traffic. Her father met her at a Dunkin Donuts where she tried to warm up a little. Her husband, Rich, had an idea. He suggested they go home, get her into fresh, warm clothes, and return to the Dunkin Donuts to finish the race. He also used his hosting job as a cohost of the Toucher and Rich sports show on the local radio station to let her friends know what was happening.

Mary finally crossed the finish line at 12:18 a.m.—thirteen hours and three minutes after starting. She was amazed to hear cheers from a group of people there at the finish line. These were her friends. And she raised over $35,000 for Dana-Farber. Will she run it again? Mary says probably not. Her desire is to volunteer during the marathon to assist runners as she found so many people there for her during her run.[37]

Mary Shertenlieb finished the race. She didn't win it. However, I would say she won something far greater than a cash prize or a medal.

NOW CONSIDER THIS

How would you define "winning" in your life?
  With whom are you competing?
  Is your understanding of God concerned with winning and losing?
  What is God urging you to take on that is a challenge to you?

---

[37] https://www.boston.com/sports/boston-marathon/2018/04/17/mary-shertenlieb-boston-marathon-finish.

CHAPTER 16

PERSISTENCE IS GOD'S WAY

The late Earle Nightingale, writer and publisher of inspirational and motivational newsletters, once told a story about a boy named Sparky. For Sparky, school was all but impossible. He failed every subject in eighth grade. He flunked physics in high school, getting a grade of zero. Sparky also flunked Latin, algebra, and English. He didn't do much better in sports. Although he did manage to make the school's golf team, he promptly lost the only important match of the season. There was a consolation match: he lost that one, too.

Throughout his youth, Sparky was awkward socially. He was not actually disliked by other students; no one cared that much. He was astonished if a classmate ever said hello to him outside of school hours. There's no way to tell how he might have done at dating. Sparky never once asked a girl to go out in high school. He was too afraid of being turned down.

Sparky was a loser. He, his classmates, everyone knew it. So he rolled with it. Sparky had made up his mind early in life that if things were meant to work out, they would. Otherwise, he would content himself with what appeared to be his inevitable mediocrity.

However, one thing was important to Sparky—drawing. He was proud of his artwork. Of course, no one else appreciated it. In his senior year of high school, he submitted some cartoons to the editors of the year book. His cartoons were turned down. Despite this rejection, Sparky was so convinced of his ability to draw that he decided to become a professional artist.

After completing high school, he wrote a letter to Disney Studios. He was told to send some samples of his artwork, and the subject for a cartoon was suggested. Sparky drew the proposed cartoon. He spent a great deal of time on it and on all the other drawings he submitted. Finally, the reply came from Disney Studios. He had been rejected once again. Another loss for the loser.

Sparky persisted, though. He decided to write his own autobiography in cartoons. He described his childhood self—a little boy loser and chronic underachiever. The cartoon character would soon become famous worldwide! This boy who had such a lack of success in school and whose work was rejected again and again was Charles Schultz. He created the *Peanuts* comic strip and the little cartoon character whose kite would never fly and who never succeeded in kicking a football—Charlie Brown.

In the church, the holy week preceding Easter is a time to remember how people often reject what God has given. In Isaiah 53, the prophet notes that the suffering servant of God was nothing to look at. Nothing about his appearance was noble or majestic. Yet God chose him to be a witness. And the response of the people? Total rejection.

Isaiah's words became the template to describe the life and rejection of the Messiah Jesus. To the world at that time, Jesus was nothing more than another crazy rabble-rouser prophesying about God. People listened to him for a time, but many grew weary and disenchanted when he didn't raise up an army to fight against Rome. In the end, they abandoned him to be arrested, beaten, and crucified as a criminal. And so, the world took no notice of another disappointing "messiah," another "loser," hanging on a cross by the side of the road.

But God wasn't through with this gift. Jesus wasn't gone. Nor are the gifts that God blesses us with every day. There's hope for the world. There's hope for you! *You* are worth so much more than you know to God. Persist!

Now Consider This

Many people loved the *Peanuts* comic strips and animated features that are still watched by people today. The persistence of Charles Schultz in believing in just one part of himself eventually made the difference in finding his niche in the world.

What is the one thing you believe in about yourself?

Are you willing—nay, are you *ready* to persist in making that belief a reality in your life today? If so, then begin your adventure, my friend!

CPSIA information can be obtained
at www.ICGtesting.com
Printed in the USA
BVHW022121151019
561163BV00012B/171/P

9 781532 083426